ISBN: 978-1-917617-16-1

Cover designed by Aaron Kent

Edited and Typeset by Aaron Kent

Broken Sleep Books Ltd
PO BOX 102
Llandysul
SA44 9BG

AFTER THE PARTING

Meier currently resides in London. She is the Chair of the Twelve Behind International Poetry Festival in China, the Editor-in-Chief of Autumn Water, a poetry journal in Taiwan and the organiser of Ruthin Art Festival in Wales, UK. Meier began publishing her poetry since 18 and has released several collections, including The Weight of a Sponge, You and Me, and Twelve Behind. Her poetry has been translated and published in over a dozen languages, including English, Russian, Japanese, German, Mongolian, Arabic, Persian, Hungarian, and Ukrainian.

CONTENTS

After The Parting

Meier

Broken Sleep Books

TWIN RIVERS KARST CAVERN

— I cannot tell you all my secrets
Because my secrets are still growing

I

The seawater rises once more,
carrying the full surge of its desire,
from the tip of the tongue to the depths of the soul.
Those creatures cannot escape.
Earth, please shelter their heroic remains—
insects, fish, even
pandas and rhinos.
Seven hundred million years from now,
people will find their fossils
and worship them like gods.

Forget my pain, repeated again and again,
and the sharp, second-hand joy.

Inside me, secrets begin to intertwine,
relaying signals from seven hundred million years ago.
I have always been alive,
like a legend.

II

I have swallowed flames
and endured fractures.
The heart-rending pain is filled with water.

That is my clear, deep blood.
The wounds no longer heal.

Stone flowers bloom everywhere,
and the fields of calcified pools, large and small,
are your terraces.
Under your sun and moon, they too blossom and bear fruit.
Your warmth is her sunlight.
Your gaze, traversing seven hundred million years of tunnels,
falls upon her, full of tenderness.

III

The stone is forgotten.
Another stone grows within it.
The stone abandons itself in another form.
The stone blooms into its own crystalline flowers.

Sometimes, the stone forgets the world outside,
light as cotton,
like rippling tenderness
piercing through hardened time.

Alone, but not lonely,
my clear, resonant voice has never sung.
Seven hundred million years of silence gleam like stars.
To wait for you, the stones guard their words like gold.

IV

When the spectacle ends,
and all the lights dim,
my heart is covered in dust.
Once-turbulent waves leave their marks on the stone.
When the flood came,
elephants and rhinos had no time to flee.

Again and again, small collapses happen within me.
Once, I held the tail of a dinosaur,
longing for a trace of warmth.
Time often overlooks the songs of trees and rain.
They cover me,
long since a part of me I cannot sever.

Villagers carrying firewood walk along my spine.
Smoke rises from chimneys.
The scent of twilight herbs, mingling with the sunset,
comforts my darkness.

They say a coin has two sides.
What difference is there
between me and my other side?

V

An eagle once tried to fly into my heart,
but its dive was too fierce.
In the limited sunlight, I store water.
Dense forests are the horizon for insects.

The never-ending waterfall
is my roaring voice.
All that I can confide—
my cylindrical body is covered in wounds.
They are my veins.
Through them, I connect
with all of you, ever-living.

The eagle flies skyward along the vertical cliff,
leaving me a heart that can soar, even in confinement.

VI

In your porcelain-like gesture,
I understand nostalgia.

Seven hundred million years of solitude and thunder
are the footsteps of your past life.
An egg multiplies on the jagged wall.
Stone and water
become a totem,
worshipped.

(05.05.2015, in flight from Zunyi to Nanjing)

ANCIENT TETHYS SEA

I

I drift on the sea, like a log
No, like a stone
Each day your salt bites deep. My skin, now scaled,
Grows tougher like stone polished by the tide
Webbing grows between my toes
Eons later I have turned into a naiad
At the cave mouth where you pass

II

Sunlight pierces my eyes
I must withdraw to depths of the earth's core
I can hear your echo
More than that, an eon ago, I was on the sea's surface
Dehydrated for want of a drop of water, which you gave me
Letting my shriveled feet breathe again
Thenceforth an accord was reached
Between one stone and another

You hid away in my heart
I forgot that I would still encounter you
An ancient augury bloomed into crystalline flowers
More diaphanous than bolls of cotton

III

I know you won't turn and leave
I've waited eons for this moment
I strive to keep my waist slender, my legs nicely shaped
I moved toward you at a snail's pace
Bringing all tears, memories, pangs and allurements
I awaited your caresses
Your absorbed gaze that sets one trembling

Afterwards, day by day, year by year
I live within your field of view
And raptly watch you in the stream of years
If only this moment does not slip by
Let it fend off the all-eroding eon to come

IV

When stones snuggle up to each other
Or complete a kiss that takes an eon of longing
Dear One, I beg you not to go far
Crossing a hidden river I'll reach that Chasm of the Creation
Then upstream past a waterfall to that Courtyard of Creation
Abloom with wildflowers, to where you gaze afar
I want to stand on your shoulders
Use your language to interpret the ocean
Teach me the grammar of waves

The ocean and the salt therein
Magnesium and moonlight that dapple Twin Rivers
The ocean and the living things therein
As well as myself, glow of sunset in the distance

V

Make a taxidermist's specimen of me
Lower a boat down from a cliff's edge
My blue hair is a flickering fire
Light, in the abyss, falls as water drops

700 million years ago I grew a tongue
In order to converse with you in this lifetime
But silence is most expressive
In your brilliant rays

VI

I can hear my own snores
A boulder lies on the boulders where you've been
Shadows overlapping, like your truths passed down orally
Have trekked...from succulence of thriving years to the present

The present is just a leaf from a tree
Or fireflies over a stretch of hilly ground
I have not dispatched so much as a mouse
To creep nonchalantly past your slumbering self
Nighttime surf as yet unstirring
Recedes behind a latticed window

Once I saw a banded krait swimming
Past a childhood riverbank. Grass blade accomplices
Transformed a rainbow-hued vow
Into an expedition route

Wandering in the earth's interior
Each crevice was once filled with seawater
Scales and armor plate were cast off layer by layer
You've seen my towering guise, my soaring guise
In order to pursue a bat
I mastered the skill of gulping down darkness

Whereupon, at present
I transform into a transparent fish
The spangles once seen along my dark back
Have turned into transparent vital organs

I watch in silence
Transformed to an ornate underground palace
A mirage you see above water
Having no quarrel with the world,
I wait

(10.09.2015 Beijing)

TWELVE BEHIND*

Preface

Your Majesty, for eons you have hidden yourself away
I come with reeling footsteps to kneel before you
All the sand deposited by whirlwinds
Has metamorphosed into crystalline pearls
Around the rims of pellucid pools

Your Majesty, you are dispersed across twelve sites
So your leopard spots can become colourful clouds
At thirty degrees north
I sit straight-backed within your heart
I become the only emerald
Found at this latitude

I

Take flight, sparks
Head far away to where birds go to die
Where spirits fly and dance over the sea
You say, Dear one, aim your weapon at me
The forest is fertile but my heart's a desert
And I cannot face its barrenness

Stand upright, Majesty, in your robe of fur
Reclaim the cave-mouths one by one
From a peak you gaze down over the ridges
Your armour bright as stars

II

Listen to that singing from the woodland
Better than those cries and howls
Angels comfort every stone
From Five-Peak Ridge to Nine Gates
Majesty, a command from you turns back
The passion of floods that know no self-restraint

When darkness gives place to dazzling blue
The Twelve Sites grow quiet
The King leaves his throne
Each winged, crawling, running creature
Possesses its own love like morning dew

III

Midnight, splitting open
Starlight splitting open
Trees and stones splitting open
Sky splitting open
All are packed into a crevice in the earth

Your Majesty, you are a dagger
Your pain triumphs over time itself
For seven hundred million years you have played the go-between
Drawing heaven and earth together
For seven hundred million years you have swallowed it all
Including, one by one, the old folk who gathered herbs
Who now appear as marvellous mountain fruits
Your promise blooms as crystalline flowers
Shimmering in caves

IV

Your Majesty, this spring seize the time before the snakes awaken
Hold me close, repair my wrinkles
Your stories spur the flowers
To compete in wonder and beauty
Looking down from sheer cliff-faces, mocking the mosses

That is your skin, your Majesty
I am hidden within it, buried in your breath
In all these back-country sites the hearts you have gathered up
Have long been taken as exemplary
I won't let you out of my sight
While a panda naps in a tree
I trade my life-blood for your soul

V

Are seeds really so important? In the bellies of birds
They take root, sprout, endure the winter
Now in full bloom as colours of springtime
Your Majesty, never have I yearned to pass through you
As I do now, pass through your glances and growth rings
To the solitude hidden deep beyond your halo

Seeds in the bottom of the frozen valley
Sun Mountain, Moon Lake
Borrow from me the shimmer of sunlit waves
To call out to you
Your Majesty, behind your achievements
Lie seven hundred million years
Of nightly silence

VI

Most of the time, of course, I am an angel
Holding an infant to my bosom in a carriage made for sprites
Applying eerie colours to this lovely life

No, most of the time I am a witch
My life has been smooth but the way I tell it
It is full of thorns, with pitfalls at every turn

I drift between flame and shadow, backwards and forwards
Because I fear I may not meet your depths again
Your Majesty, on your collars I see my codes embroidered
At thirty degrees north I stand at a primitive crossroads
Keeping company with forests and caves
I worship the dust beneath your feet

(11.03.2016, In flight from Zunyi to Beijing)

**The Twelve Back Country Sites is a scenic area containing remarkable geological and natural features, located in Suiyang County, Guizhou Province. The scenic area includes several natural wonders: Twin Rivers Cavern National Geologic Park, Qingxi Gorge and Tong-Oil Creek Subterranean Crevice.*

GUIYANG

I. Cold Rain

This is how tracks are made
The chill steamrolls my skin
Still a long way from the gap between seasons
And when surveyed from a high-rise building
Certain ties of feeling seem indefinite

So what is to be done?
The sleeping lotus already died in summer
Guiyang is colder than the temperature of my soul's breath
I keep losing my way, or losing my calm in heavy traffic

It's a matter of distance between spells of cold rain
You and I are separated by glass
From a good many mountains and rivers away
Comes an awakening tap at your window

II. Labels

Upon my face you planted
Seeds of a great many wishes
I expound on the highland's taken-for-granted wilderness
As I clutch the arm of a wormseed plant

There comes a time I too feel numb
Amid jostling, faceless throngs
And the fizz of real estate prices
Those who feel cut off and threatened
Band together to warm each other

I belong under an alternative label
In a market north of Guiyang, where purple potatoes abound
I appear as a voodoo lily*
Bowing in the sun, renamed, unrooted.

III. The Southland in Chilly Weather

The southland is curled up among petals
Fallen leaves go ransacking about
Through a frozen energy field, but cannot find
Last year's voluptuous lips
Memories of rime-ice persist
The nation bemoans a snowed-in mountain district
Fallen electric poles are sheathed in ice

A thousand islands where bracket fungus and bean vines grew
A thousand southlands, dressed in sunlight
Dressed in garments of violet cornflowers
Their music scrambled, played by disordered fingers

Southland, an insoluble knot hidden in my heart
No matter how cold, was a place warmed by my fingertips
Do not trespass the jungle where my blood ran wild
I am in Guiyang and have forgotten the world's center

IV. To the North

Forget those honors
Most are bound up with affliction
Those teeth atop a megalith

Were a kingdom in remote antiquity
Guiyang and a domain further north
Were founded then

You have entered my body
Like a tree always planted on yonder hillside

(21.01.2016, Empark Grand Hotel, Guiyang)

[1] Amorphophallus konjac, also called konjac or voodoo lily, is grown in Southwest China and Japan for its starchy edible root bulb. The flower of the konjac blooms facing the sun.

AFTER THE PARTING

After the parting, no one tends my wounds—
Winds howl, the moon drowns, trees twist in the tide.
I climb your left ear—a cliff of shattered noons.
Sunflowers kneel, their gold gone thin and wide.

The sun still bleeds, van Gogh.
Your cheeks: two caves where time chews its own bones.
Eyes—black wells where the sky throws its stones.

Don't paint. Don't walk the fields—
The soil heaves drunk, wild mugwort chokes the air.
After the parting, no one tends my wounds—

Your beard's storm swallows the sea's despair.
Brushstrokes snap—the lady's spinning skirt
a noose of snakes, their heads now bare,
black roses in the whirlwind's glare.

Don't go to Arles. Don't wake the wheat!
Apple's core, core's sun—
a bullet lodged where heartbeats meet:
love's last arrow left undone.

van Gogh, I'm the yellow that stains their eyes,
nailed to the sun's wheel,
spun by their cries. After the parting,
sunflowers steal where we kneel.

Yet no one
tends me.

January 15, 2020, afternoon, London

THE COLOURFUL COLD

I

Now, my arms hang limp,
my back aches, and of course,
so does the heart hidden in my ribs.
I can't feel her breath.
The wind comes from the north,
from Mongolia, Xinjiang, Russia,
even from the icy cracks of the Arctic.
I lie there like a collapsed bell,
like Dalí's time,
slumped on the edge of a bathtub,
a glass of red wine clutched in my hand.

This is no blue depression—
my back is covered in whirlpools,
footprints filled with water.
I will never forgive those gasps,
without climax, like a train without brakes,
rolling aimlessly across borders.

Beetles spread their beautiful wings.
Paintings peek out
from derelict factories and rusted frames,
laughing with eerie voices.

My hair is always gray, always messy.
The guitar returns to its place as a huqin.
The White-Haired Girl lets out a sob,
and the grand opera ends.

The banquet begins in the cold.

II

Once again, I consult the pipe,
this naked prison.
When two eyes cannot focus,
a split skull, a split life, and smoke
are the only certain truths.

Sunflowers, pyramids, yaks,
phalluses, compasses, pipes in mouths—
no one starts from themselves,
and few ever reach themselves.

Outside the vegetarian restaurant, business thrives.
Great clusters of snowflakes, like the robes of the I Ching,
extend fate in a blur.
By the time you truly awaken,
everything has already melted.

III

The weathered oyster, as vivid as when alive,
rough seawater, cracks,
the pleasure of lips and tongue.
When sea meets shore,
hooks and ropes conspire.
Light is on the mountain, on its peak.
Crows are as cold as the night.
Colorful stones split in midair.
Knowledge sits cross-legged, changing tones.
The drag queen is male.

The morbid dance, waist down, weeping,
waist up, calmly insane.

798, art in the dust,
an era and its sorrows that cannot be brushed away.
Flesh and soul, reality and dream,
night and night, stripped from form to flesh.

IV

Those awls, mouths agape,
baring teeth, outdated fixations
passed off as avant-garde. Braids are in fashion.
The soil, trampled, drinks its fill of paint.
The masters float by, expressionless.

I see piles of garbage,
piles of garbage brimming with wisdom.
Starlight flickers among them.
Piles of curses,
piles of creation,
piles of nothingness,
piles of tears, piles of fruit
rotting to the core.

Piles of heartache,
from 7 to 9, then to 8.
Piles of the future
clog reality, leaving no way out.

V

This cold empties space,
starting from the river. History forgets to weep.
Shadows, in Rome, the Colosseum,
call out to Beijing, Beijing's descendants, Beijing's whores.
The palace, its splendor and strife, like Caesar
fallen in a pool of blood.
From 7 to 9, back to 8,
back to the earth's core,
where nothing remains.

(01.01.2016, in flight)

** White Fur Maiden is the title of a Peking opera first performed in 1945 and remade as a popular movie in 1950. It tells the story of Xi-er, a young peasant woman who was abducted and forced to work in an evil landlord's household. After running away she was cared for by beasts in the mountains, causing her hair to turn white. Eventually she took revenge.*

*** 798 Art District was formerly an industrial zone in northeast Beijing. In preparation for the Olympic Games, the city encouraged development of a world-class art destination by approving the conversion of pre-existing buildings into art centers, galleries, and artists' studios during the 1990s. Many design companies and cultural enterprises also set up offices there. By the early 2000s, 798 was the most thriving art district in Beijing.*

**** According to numerology of the Book of Changes, 7 stands for "unchanging yang" and 9 stands for "changing yang" (also called "old yang"). The number 8 stands for "unchanging yin." Thus the numbers 7-9-8 symbolize a progression from yang to yin. Coincidentally these numbers are found in the name of "798 Art District."—Translator*

FLOWERS OF RUIN

I

Salt grows out of the ground
Dawn blooms into a shapeless lotus
I am suspended next to your lips
A silent stone, I am your angel
Transformed into part of you

Salt dissolves into stone, hangs in trees
Snowflakes of the spirit, powerless hands
I entrust my life force to this pair of feet
Henceforth the world cannot be relied on

Let me return to your side, to reckless kisses
Experiencing density through your texture
You are my grand nullity
Crystalline, yielding flowers that grow
From my luscious flesh
I am the reason you go on existing
700 million years, I am
Your ruins, true and beautiful

II

Henceforth the geomantic dial traverses the land
With pearls resembling an angel's tears
A fissure in simple time becomes a black hole
Baby black hole...inflation...cosmos
Cycling through lifetimes in a formula...I twist a lock of hair
As I take leave of planet earth

Leaving you, I leave bamboo overgrown with thorn-bushes
Transparent water lilies, a pure-proud heart
I wrap up half a lifetime of tender affinity
Go knocking on some other planet

There at a successful turn in the road
I ran into my other self amid ruins
Such purity as hers would cause jealousy
And so, in the name of conventionality
I fight a duel with her

III

If it comes to blades bared in shadows, making ready to pounce
I have crouching tigers and hidden dragons up my sleeve
My other self's smile hides arcane intrigues
Stones, gems in vibrant colors
Roll past melancholy's dark blue

I and myself have been forgiven by god
I and myself cannot take each other's place
A reed-bed near the house, azaleas up on the mountain
From springtime I get a special peek at truth
Truth is elsewhere

I am born anew, amid ruins
And am relentlessly ridiculed by my other self

IV

Leopard, water and grassland
All those details you range over
Calcify into hardened time
Deep down in Chasm of Creation surges a hidden river
I am a grain of dust that does not settle
Floating past a plantain's luxuriant years

The traces you left on stone
Long ago turned to a fossil
So I must go to a pompous museum
To see crinoids pricked by stern lights
The unwithering rose is a myth
Here on the other side of the glass
My heart is swimming in tears

V

In the midst of a sumptuous banquet
When the flood comes
Ants have to time to move house
Insects and winged creatures hold mid-air revels
A cow cannot stand, its vision dizzied
The wood's grain yields to decay

Choppy passages of time
Transform to a stretch of sea salt
I am the origin of a myriad things, which come from dust
And finally return to dust

(09.12.2015, night, Twin Rivers)

FROM TODAY ONWARD

I

From today onward, I am a piece of rope from your stable
In order to perform tonsure on sweet-scented grass
I keep watch all night under the stars
Waiting for your footsteps in the moonlight

Rain of thirty years ago stops in mid-air
That figure on the exercise ground is me running barefoot
The luminosity of all created things drips from the hem of your shirt
As for beams that radiated from my crystalline feet of jade
You give them back to me tonight, Twin Rivers

I grew to be your woman, your consort
In the prime years of life I occupied your palace
What I write on the sky's curtain
You have already read between my breasts

II

From today onward, Twin Rivers
Lifting my skirt hemmed with helictites
I sit erect to reign as unassuming queen
My humility strewn amid flowers and herbs
Will perform rites to sun and moon for me

Don't let me shed tears for hardship
That I endured on the road to this rendezvous

They have been carefully stowed in crevices
Including my wrenching grief in Jerusalem
The curses and thorns I hurled at Jesus
My cleansing has changed it all to moonlight for you

What we have not comprehended of each other
Will be left to sit facing the ranged mountains
To join the immortals in solitude

III

Scales of skin peel and fall from my feet*
Those are from the purse seine of my heart
If not to stay away from the danger of swords
Why would I assume this semblance of ironwork?

Why would I sink like a feather in water
Watching immature doves expound on peace foolishly?
This world exists...in an outward-radiating formula
The illusion of nesting layers
Begins with the paralysis of Steven Hawking

IV

Those shadows on the threshing ground—I must push them forward
Only then can I stay clear of the coming storm
Purple mulberries stain my teeth
I sit erect beneath a tree, in a chess game with light and shade

In your hand is a slingshot, and you push back a green bough
As you pass through the neighboring shade
Your peripheral sight scans the scenery here
Chrrrr of cicadas, song of hoped-for sunshine

As wisps of cooking smoke rise at twilight
A smell of hay pervades the air
Dogs conclude their joyous barks of pursuit
I return to the heart that knows sweet potatoes
And watch the moonlight, inch by inch
Spread over a haystack a young man's face

V

You and I were fated to meet anew after 30 years
Like my encounter with Byron on a footbridge in Lausanne
That twilight hour, the prisoner of Chillon was still surrounded by water
I walked to Montreaux...My fingers twirling a maple leaf
All the way from autumn to winter

Byron was scudding across Lac Léman
The ardor of his blood could engulf a fortress
Those muted chants and intonings
The ceaseless noise of crashing waves
Were suffused with his enduring brilliance

Back to your embrace, Twin Peaks
From today onward, your cold is my cold
I merge with stone, as if by god's covenant
Return to dust
Return to the time of nothingness

(29.01.2016, before dawn, Guiyang)

* *The image of scaly feet resonates with the myth of Great Yu, who tamed waterways with prodigious labor. According to mythology, Great Yu was a culture hero who drained swamps, cleared river channels, and vanquished titan-like beasts (in the manner or Hercules). Because he spent so much time standing in water, his legs grew scales like a fish or dragon. While engaged in his work he passed his own house several times but was too busy to enter.*
—Translator

WITHIN AND BEYOND A GLANCE

String words yet unspoken on a long thread
Cover you up with a fallen leaf
Within a prescribed circle delve into the human essence

Moonlit waves crash against a shoal
There is no corral for the heart
Within or beyond
No season can hold our full measure
So I conceal my smile amid dancing tree shadows

I must become a part of things
Make that homburg-wearing sage love me
Then throw away the door jamb
Become a planet-wide adventuress

This gaze has a starting place but no end point
For the sake of a meaningless requital
Bodies of water have flowed over these shoulders
I crawl to the point of becoming an earthworm
Contracting and expanding
Uneasily in the lap of earth

(1989)

OLDEST UNCLE

Oldest Uncle walks feebly on a path between fields
In front of him is a flock of healthy sheep
Or a raft of ducks showing iridescent feathers
Or a gray, melancholy mule
He fits well with them in a painter's rural scene
Along with ants that are familiar with his cough

Folks say Oldest Uncle was a handsome, strong young man
He beat Auntie black and blue
For her disgraceful behavior
But there came a season when he began wheezing
For twenty years he wheezed like an endless wind
One day our shrewish Auntie chased him with a pole
He scrambled for his life around the village pond
Amid scenes of gawkers and offended willow trees
That would remind him of his miseries

Water in the pond went from clear to murky
In the end it faded away like a story
Along with bright stars over the threshing ground
One evening he was blocked from going further
By a gob of phlegm that rose in his throat
His fingernails left downward scratch-marks on a wall
Oldest Uncle's hunched-over life
Was like his breath that always came in gasps
Pale and covered with patches

(1991)

ROYAL SCION

—Dedicated to my child who made a fleeting appearance in this world

You were a spotless white lotus
A crystalline bloom in my puddle of blood
That night all brilliance was eclipsed by your descent

You are daintily laid out in holy light
My heart's flower dais took 30 years to cultivate
For you I trimmed a flowering bough for 30 years
It took me 30 years preparing a road
Just to greet your little, little life

Yet your mother was once a fleet-footed deer
Each day her fervent running warmed the ground
Where sun shone brightly on green grass
Not knowing that the city's foul vapors
Were contending against the air we breathed
And so in this urban civilization
I carelessly let you slip away

Royal scion
All grass seeds that were interred that night
Heard a heart-rending wail
Your mother is a foolish speckled deer
Give me a river   Lord
I am terribly thirsty

Your dark brown eyes and finely shaped hands
Were lamps for saying farewell that dark night
In a baptismal hymn
All birds, beasts and tiny creatures
Sang in praise of of your fleeting advent

(December 1999)

A DESOLATE ENCOUNTER—MACCHU PICCHU

I

Who stepped on my chest, leaving it sore?
I sit on your throne,
reading a tale of a kingdom no more.

Stones, silent and heavy as iron,
bear the weight of hammers swung,
striking the void where Cusco's hopes are gone.
Gold may never die,
but it cannot buy your life.
The king sits frozen, trembling in a frame,
facing helmets and horses, Europe's cruel game.

Melancholy flows through Cusco's panpipe song.
You cannot grasp the civilization wronged.
The Sun God falls, his power undone.
Now, the age of suffering has just begun.

II

The alpaca's people are gentle and kind—
a gentle bitterness,
sap from coca leaves, a bitter grind.
The plateau's songs, vast and blue as the sky,
echo as I gallop, asking why
this Eastern woman dares to dream
of saving your ruin, a futile scheme.

III

A song climbs the mountain,
Machu Picchu,
your seams soaked in wine.
Mudslides roar, a grand design,
while sun and moon in vastness shine.

Named stones dance beneath the night.
Once, you reveled in the mountain's might,
with a thousand concubines in your sight.
Machu Picchu!

From the stones, desolate blood flows.
Cusco's cathedral bells now repose.
Above the sun, the moon's heart bleeds,
trampled by hooves, it silently pleads.

I touch your pain, a witch disgraced,
and tears fall, my sorrow traced.

IV

Now I face the snow, calm and still,
as it falls, a shroud, a chill,
hiding the sword of a kingdom's ill.

The sky grows wild, overrun with weeds.
Cusco, closer to the sun, concedes,
its voice silenced by snowy deeds.

V

Destroy a church—no, a temple's grace—
and the plateau falls, the heart's high place.
Destroy the fire struck from stone,
destroy the air, thin and alone.

The immortal octave's timeless song—
within the stones, where mortise and tenon belong—
endures a desolation, ancient and strong.

VI

Pull fire from your chest,
from the Andes' crest.
How many eagles has that skull fed?
When even they rot, this embrace is dead.

Mysterious Urubamba, your passion flows,
reaching the peak where once joy rose.
A mountain range, a starlit face,
the Intihuatana stone in its place.
Three windows:
sun, moon, woman's grace.

Gather every pilgrim's heart,
adding to the dust, a work of art.
Machu Picchu,
you can no longer face the sun alone.
Your soul, disturbed, from the gods has flown.

VII

A child races the train, a resilient root,
Inca blood, a timeless pursuit.
Pale space, hardened time,
Neruda's horse, Bingham's chime.

Before the stones, all turns to sand,
decaying grains slip through the hand.

Three windows:
time, space, alpaca's stand.

VIII

Andes, your black trains and faces stare,
black rainforests cradle light so rare.
Andes, you plunge into a valley's stream,
a rushing force, a mountain's dream.
You stand, a mirror, rough and sheer,
for four hundred years, you hide the rain's cheer,
letting the mountains forget, year by year.

Time is not yours to command.
It builds, then destroys, with a ruthless hand.

IX

Pascuti, the last Inca king, foresaw
people sifting through history's raw
ashes to find the stone's mottled flaw.

Words' secrets hide in a mountain's maw.
The blood of a fallen kingdom,
smeared on stone bread, a solemn hymn.

Women nourished these lands,
and at Machu Picchu, they made their stands,
sacrificed to a sun's false commands.

X

No redemption truly arrives—
not gold, temples, or church hives,
not time, space, or cosmic drives,
not lambs, women, or angelic lives.

Machu Picchu,
you watch Cusco's prosperity grow,
falling into the world's homogenized show.
You can only offer silence,
loneliness, ruins, and defiance,
weaving lies for prayers' reliance.

XI

Yes, open my wound,
open the Inca's tomb,
open Peru's, South America's gloom,
open the world's consuming womb!

Open the unrecorded slaughter,
open the desert's dust-choked water,

open a heart, bleeding and bare,
open the stones' pain, night's despair!

Open that land, starved of air,
its seeds, pure, without compare.
In the wound, they will grow,
slowly, surely, a resilient glow.

XII

There is no nirvana, no final rest.
In the year's last month, a winter's test,
you enter summer, a fiery quest.

This desolate encounter, tightly spun,
woven with bamboo, needle, and thread,
becomes my eyelids, my lashes' spread.
In a blink, the world is undone.

On your weathered cheek,
my trembling fingerprint speaks—
a mark of this life, eternal, unique.

(17.11.2014, Los Angeles)

WORDS OF MOURNING

Whose house is that sparrow from, flying in smoky mist?
One could take it for a knife, slicing at the margins of years
The flowers are so gorgeous they surpass imagination
Another world, a stove belly, an entrance-way
Suppose a degree of earnestness summoned by final breaths
Drifting threads would part from the inmost marrow
Those twinges of pain...would be walled off
Leaving a bounding river, to be blocked by mounds of dirt
The soil and the soil's heart
Would slowly turn dry

This was an ending, a full circle, an over-leaping
Of coastal and open seas, watched by a houseful of progeny
A lifetime of tough resolve turned to nothing, and blessings
Are hardly different from the noisy fanfare next door
Form takes precedence over content

Return to those sounds of vibrant laughter
The one lying there...knows better than anyone else
Falling asleep...is only continuing to live in another way
But even more rationally, more in love with solitude
No longer disturbed by coarseness of matter or spirit
As for the finest weapon, the choice has always been silence
From this end to that
From west to east

(27.09.2017, in flight, Guiyang-Beijing)

JOHN FORBES NASH

I am partial to the realities you hallucinated
So truthfully that they played a part
In structuring your life's equation

If certain numbers, punctuation marks, symbols
Were indeed to slip down from your open window
And seize the mechanism that makes glass explode
Then your classroom desk, the layers of calculated years
Would all, in the hysterical thrill of that sunny afternoon,
Be dashed to pieces, yet you would neither be sad nor happy

The air is liberated

Imagined harm renews your sense of guilt
You gamble with yourself, in your self-discovery
Wine and coffee dance wildly together
Later they tell you, in political, military and trade negotiations
You are there in the thick of it, like the best of overt operatives
You have influenced the refinement of variables, the precision of missiles

Yet on the dais, in Nobel's Stockholm
You had only one pair of eyes, one heart, and had only one message
Love is part of the making of reality
As for wraiths, they go on gaming with you
You give them a glance, but turn away again
And stride out through the door

(27.09.2017, in flight, Guiyang-Beijing)

PRAGUE

Water of prophecy overflows the threshold
Out of a princess's hat grows a blade of grass
Through the eyes of love, it doesn't matter
If a glass of wine at dead of night sets the stars reeling

A fairy tale lives in a castle, a witch on a cliff-edge
Spreads magical wings, all the bells
Peal in sequence, at the city's centre the twelve apostles
Offer, as always, empty handfuls, take the stage promptly
A performance of sorrowful redemption
Is tossed from the window

Rain falling on Charles Bridge
An imposing prison releases doves
Golden Lane where good is separated from evil
At the centre, in the cathedral
This argument has continued for a thousand years

Vltava River enumerates your brilliancies
Those statues transfixed by time
Take on history's sentiments, as under night's canopy
A sword that slashed time and flowing water
Now sleeps on the shore

No matter how K disguised himself, a land surveyor
Is sure to find seeds in an attic
A beetle under a desk or
The unbearable lightness of being under a glaring sun

Sure to find timeless love, Kafka and me
Prague, at that moment igniting
Red embers falling on rooftops
And in every household the sound of soulful songs

(29.09.2017, late night, Beijing)

BORN ANEW

A butterfly's wings flutter in errant course
Once the end of days comes, the Lord's work begins
Another kind of lamp...nurses the present moment
Moon...waxes only to wane, from crescent to full
People...gather only to part, from with to without
Words of parting drown out rainfall, and dreams
Are like spells of rain, rills gather to flood...
A day later....limpid like at the beginning

Of course you occupy the major part of a day's time
Heartaches like quicksilver
Tattoo of hoof beats in Africa
I cohabit with a pristine tree
Light of the Holy Spirit shines between us
I hold no expectations of miracles, but a miracle
Is here with me, from breadth of rangeland
To each fondly pining cell
Love has gone through its crazy course
I cannot give you my hand, because
A fingernail sold out my yesterday, and yesterday
Now hides within a heap of old possessions
Silent and unspeaking

(05.10.2017 late night, Huaian)

CONFESSION IN FRESH FLOWERS

Life is passed in relay, root and flower
Pangs of suffering at separation
Jade fallen low, jade rated as worthless
Jade erased from its owner's memory
Jade, continuing to enrich life, and life
No longer knows where it's going

Fresh flowers...this moment's confession
When all kisses have become memories
Those tears that usher them forth
Crawl in a riverbed, where leaves
Block the sunlight

A horse...is munching on fresh flowers
The sky...is growing dim

(05.10.2017, late night, Huaian)

BEDTIME STORY

Different seasons bloom in one flower
A lamp's shadows linger
Wine and singing cover up
The night's expansive loneliness
A fat man sits among heaps of crabmeat
Quivering all over with glee, with side dishes of beauty

A dog decked out in gaudy feathers
An emblem of the clash of salt and flesh
A glass poured full of time is the sun and moon out there
Tonight, forgiving a bout of debauchery
Is like forgiving the rose that wilts in the early hours

And so, the ravished leaf can be repaired
Tears and air are fresh and crystal clear
Purity is a hat that doesn't know where to turn
So just pretend, pretend as hard as you can
Wear disguises so the world can't recognise you
Come here to be born again

There is no door that goes back to the past
A flower-like hand, as delicate as jade
Is your only means of fighting poison with poison
Bedtime stories have only just begun

(10.10.2017, early morning, Nanjing)

BELIEF

What kind of wasteland must you go through, before
People stop treating you like a weed of the wastes?
How steep a path must you finish walking, before...
You can cherish the scents along a thoroughfare?

What straying road of intoxication
Warms your features like a balmy wind?
Having shouted yourself hoarse...in silence
There is a whole world at last

A wheat kernel beset by cold and hunger
Covets a life of blessings
When an automobile runs over a star
That which dies is a cosmos
That which lives anew is a ladder of light

(11.10.2017, before dawn, Huaian)

A GATE FOR SHEEP

When all the clouds are blown through the same mountain gap
And the growling lion unleashes his fury
The flock of sheep must pass along a cliff-edge
A gate is open wide

Facile faith goes riding on camels
Moses's staff strikes out at rock, at the flock of sheep

When your face is wet with tears
And all gateways are blocked, you cannot
Glean happiness from betrayal
Under olive trees in the Garden of Gethsemane
Your gate is the gate for sheep to pass through
The sheep's gate is your gate
No one knows that in the wilderness
Where cup after cup once brimmed
There has been nothing for a long time

(13.10.2017, afternoon, Huaian)

REVISITING PAST HAUNTS

—for my alma mater

That was an island left to itself, to thrumming crickets
And chirping birds, where one could make a life
A soprano's coloratura used to drift by from the music building
The sky...was in a trance of colors
From numbers to novels, our youthfulness
Vied in displays of beauty, while our hearts' crimson stirrings
On the way from clapboard classroom to bare practice ground
Exuded oceanic scents, a savor of peas
And peanuts, while scenes outside the walls
Allowed the expansion of youthful fantasies
We had not stripped ourselves bare, or perhaps
Lotus buds were not ready to bloom...infatuations
Were so unripe...they left an enduring aftertaste

Now the timeworn facades look like faded shoes
Ferry routes to the island have changed again and again
We traced our way back, not to determine our direction
Fish still swim here, the water is not what it used to be
The bank is still that soil, those reeds, that blankness
Of time having passed by quickly

Leaves go whirling across the sky, a southern tycoon
Makes a brief landing here, and I review you
In my heart, then dust you off
And fold you among creases...nothing can replace
The warmth you gave me

I pass by lightly, like wind on any day
Unlikely to be noticed

(20.10.2017, Huaian)

INTOXICATION

Upon raising my glass, what I fling
Toward the Great Progenitor...merely bold pronouncements

Yet grain grows in the fields again
To be greeted by painful blows of hailstones
What fills the glass must be more than gaiety and laughter
Those weighed-down journeys lose all savor
Due to vertigo, and the next day
Again you find a brand-new trough, filled
With green grass of spring; upon being reaped, the grain
Concludes its lifetime expectations
Such is not the case for life itself, which each grain crop
Becomes a part of, time after time
Like this hangover, piercing me to the quick

Sweet, sour, bitter, spicy...all in these morning-after ruins
You stand above the sea, face a cold wind head-on

Nobody cares about the toughness of a plant
Just as nobody can make out tears in the rain
Spring over a cloud-top, trailing your long sleeves
Screen that nice, round moon off from sharp edges

(10.10.2017, wee hours, Huaian)

NOT BEING A FISH

—for Danjin Rabjai

The desert is covered with snow
Your native place, a house in the wind
Tibetan language and the Buddha, the Buddha and your future lives...
No step you took ever betrayed them, like Tsangyang Gyatso
(So your troubadourage was filled with tears and heartache)
You kept receiving signals from the sun
Each morning, hints of laughter in dewdrops

All constellations can be contained in 108 stupas
Which were your cosmos, red soil and stones
We laid on the ground, our hearts open to sacred presence
Waiting for a fish to leap from the ocean
We closed our eyes, heard a far horse neigh in answer to your call

We wondered about your life, as your latter-day countrymen do
The riddle has no answer, your verses meant for the ages
Gave way to your faith, and your faith gave way
After you disappeared strangely, to love

Indeed the sea went dry, and the snows of years to come
Would whirl in sunlight, the fish would roam through snow
Leopards on pilgrimage would come and knock at the gate
A horse would serve you best, in the hour of your rendezvous
By maintaining sufficient silence

And so we understand buckthorn, all those flowers
Descending to earth, until the native place
Was virtually an ocean of flowers, strewn over grassy hills

Energy...from the sky's highest reaches
Was imparted to the sun, and then to the grassland
And to the fish...only found in dreams

Breathing in water

[Note: Danjin Rabjai was a legendary figure in Mongolian Lamaism, similar to the romantic poet Tsangyang Gyatso of Tibet. Danjin Nabujie possessed a broad range of talents, and his works of poetry and music circulated widely. The Danjin Nabujie Monastery, built at his birthplace, is a pilgrimage site. It is said that if a visitor lays down there, he or she will receive spiritual empowerment.]

PRINCESS GROOM ALLEY*

Sachet balls were tossed for white horses day after day**
In the end none were greeted with a warm-hearted button
Crabtrees bloomed and then shed, shed and then bloomed
Indoors I visualize our hometown...think about twelve years of warmth
You had, and twelve years of worldly ways, blowing hot and cold

"Force of character, personal charm, forbearance, tireless labor"
Could sum up your half century of selfless service, but can't sum up
The power of mountains and rivers in your heart, so it all comes back
To your starting place, to Princess Groom Alley, and it takes us
To your Shaoxing family tree, to the old-time robes you sent off
Broken to pieces by old China's ways

What I read here is much more
Than your distinguished service, your songs of the Yangtze broken off
To probe the secrets of diverse fields, more than sojourns in Japan and Lyon,
Your tender-heartedness and resignation
I don't know how to sing your praises, for I know
What you wanted was always more than praise songs

Princess Groom Alley at dawn, my grandfather coughs
And Mother grows frail, at Winter Solstice, you went to pay respects
To your master, no one stole a look, no sound of an imperial groom
Reciting classics, then from little roof-tiles of the Southland...slipped outside
All the way down the   River

Dou-e, the courtesan who died for love, is off at the magistrate's court again
The historical town downstream is repairing Emperor Qianlong's gazebo
Your rucksack is packed for your trip to the Northeast

Your head turns for a last look at your loved ones, in Princess Groom Alley
It will take years for people in your hometown to know
What deep purport was to be read in that glance

(14.12.2017, night, Beijing)

**Premier Zhou Enlai was born in Princess Groom Alley, Huaian City, Jiangsu Province. He left his native place at age twelve and never returned.*

***In the region south of the Yangtze, embroidered balls filled with dried herbs were tossed at weddings, to predict who would be the next to marry. A woman's offer to sew buttons was a stage in the progress of courtship.*

HOURGLASS

Right from that moment, sands and stormy events of an era
Pass through the throat
An ancient road, from nothing to something
Time, from birth to death
Even as the broadsword lifts, hope's silken threads are on their way
With one defiant howl, a life is spared beneath the blade
Even the hourglass misses a breath

This won't gauge the length of yearning, though a life
Is similar in having a start and finish...you trickle in silence
The span of a lover's gasp...like a missed heartbeat, fallen through
Fulfilling the most impossible vows
Down below...gets deeper and deeper...in the next instant
Time's flow reverses...it begins again

(14.11.2017 evening, Beijing)

WINTER SOLSTICE

The awning-covered boat is simply a stuffed dumpling
Shaoxing is fermenting its winter batch...from grain
To fine wine on the table, from south to north
The west wind becomes the north wind

The crabtree is done blossoming...plum blossoms are on the way
From today, water ices over...ground turns frozen
Daylight hours are given over to nighttime, the koala
Begins to hibernate, and pine cones in the north
Are all on their own, underneath the tree

(08.11.2017, Zunyi)

IN WRITINGS WE SEE THE FACE

Real and implied distance keeps us from meeting face to face
A leaf hesitates in the wind, the earth has ways to hurry it along
The mailbox is becoming an antique, where to deposit a heart?
Ice builds up thick layers
Snow is flurrying by now in Siberia
Winter...in its writings I see its face

The quantity of lies is equal to earnest smiles
Trickery is stretched across the Milky Way
Truths we reveal are merely a game of God
The password you know is also a barrier gate
A thousand calculations, ten thousand efforts bring something in reach
Then you take one false step...*Ah* Lord
In His writings we see His face

Spring winds are balmy, time for living things to bloom
Love begins its stealthy growth, tears their stealthy dripping
In your joys and sorrows no one can take your place
Daughter...in her writings I see her face

Parents and lovers, in their writings I see their faces
Love, hate, fondness and enmity...the Great Dao acts with utter simplicity
In its writings we see its face
Those unforeseeable endings and beginnings
In their writings we see their faces

(18.11.2017)

SUNSET OVER THE MEDITERRANEAN

That ball of fire sitting on the lap, beyond yonder mountain
Blazes up, like the soul-scorching flames over E-Fang Harem
That went rolling through Chang'an
Their mirages appear over the sea
Mediterranean waters...lapping against Nice
Blueness of the far coastline

The sun still warms Montpelier
Yesterday Lyons appeared as if in a dream
Cathedral, rocks, ancient fortress
The statuesque curves of a handsome waiter
All in fire, with silhouettes captured by Monet one morning
Ships, masts, stillness and coughing sounds upoN rising
Merge in an oceanic flood, this morning
Burning just like Picasso, and my new planting
Of plantains, their heavy leaves drooping
We have no reason to believe that the sun
Has fallen into the ocean

NIGHT MARKET / FISHERMAN'S BASTION

There are no fish, just airborne lampshades riding broomsticks
Fresh flowers lend warmth to a windy Christmas
A thin-legged mantis clings to an eave, and artists
Move their hand-crafted hours to a marketplace
The Danube River offers music...the Vitava provides boatmen
Fishermen out of work since the Middle Ages somehow built a fortress
An exquisite composition in colors, gradually
Turns into an antique

The net is flung into the stormy realm of dust, the Lord calls on the phone
No one answers. Hunyadi Matyas pushed into the heart of Austro-Hungary*
Repenting fish kneel everywhere on the riverbank
Shrimp and crabs that couldn't come ashore...love that was mired underwater
Are revealed in a thoughtfully sewn-on button, a mere leaf
There is a sword you must buy
For it has to do with dignity and slaughter and coursing white steeds
It is for palaces...your studio cannot hold it

Of course that also goes for the helmets of fishermen
And other figments of nothing in the Bastion

(28.11.2017, before dawn, Paris

** Hunyadi Matyas (1443-1490) was the Hungarian king who forged the political identity and geographical boundaries of his nation.*

BREAKFAST

The fields show scenes of rich harvest
The cherry tomato* has been cut open, lies prone across the hills
A new-grown leaf, slipping past dew-moistened lips
Sticks onto a dairy cow's shoulder, and grain kernels
Having passed through a horse's trough, break down in a culvert
Olives, coffee and cow's horns thread their way
Through a grove of trees, all morning until noon

Passing hours stroll between countries
Scandals transmitted by birds are like this glass of juice
Celery, mango, orange and carrot
Mingle in a reality that has no bloodline
Too much sweetness or salt is hard to stomach
So have a cup of tea, clear up a few sentences

Change the location and light
Wheat is separated from soil, a whole day's food
Is packed in capsules, and the fragrances
Are pinned onto the chest like flowers
From the skin of a kiwi,** climb up
All the way to a red bayberry's mouth***

(11.11.2017, morning, in flight, Budapest-Paris)

**The Chinese word for "cherry tomato" is shengnv-guo, which literally means "female-saint fruit."*

***, ***The Chinese word for "kiwi fruit" is mihou-tao, which literally means "monkey peach." The Chinese word for "red bayberry" is yang-mei, which literally means "goat poplar."*

FROM PRAGUE TO BUDAPEST

The moment a gust descends upon the crown of my head
Geometrical jigsaw pieces pass in and out
Colors from crafts in the marketplace climb onto glass
Two people lay claim to one seat, and so
The plane will be stopped from flying

From Prague to Budapest
More history is left out than mountains between the two rivers
There were more battles and carts than wheat
On the Vitava and the Danube, food is brought
From the Lord's place in dual flows, between them lies Vienna
With elegance on a huge scale, while we are satisfied

With external forms, watching a fire from the opposite bank...
Seeing a time-ravaged empire...hoodlums of East Europe muscling in
Charms of Latin America remain in Trujillo's square
Turning a corner, an Incan descendant
Scans our Oriental features, then lowers his eyes
From Prague to Budapest, Chinese silk
Has been woven onto a sheep's back; the cloth swatch we take away

Is only the shell of this stretch of river
Those obstinate, somber faces
Raise the lid of an empire; a big fogbank
Descends as if poured...our Motherland is troubled
By "sadistic brats" and "relocations," yet after terrible winds
The sky is turning clear

Instead of bridges we have links, which are becoming the sole topic
If all bridges were dismantled, Alibaba's Ma Yun would go crazy
And Tencent would cause obstructions, because when you virtualize
The ties between heart and heart, then morality
Becomes a condiment, such as
Chili peppers in the East, cheese in the West

From Prague to Budapest
The proof of cheese is in the eating

(27.11.2017, afternoon, in flight, Budapest-Prague)

THE VANISHED SEA

The part going upward from the spire's tip...has to do with God
The clang of bells lives in the interior
Prague likes music that slips into niches in the ear
Vitava River
The lower body goes downward, mire of desire
No coral in sight

The fortified tower is not a graveyard
Another kind of memorial, affording views of the city wall
You can't evade the great sea's existence
Beginning with King Charles, each statue resembles a fish
Along the route fish take, bridges are water

Savor of the mundane realm: something crystalline exudes an icy scent
Reflected beams illumine a transparent world
Don Juan gets to meet John Lennon
A man with wives and a crowd and a glass factory*
Break down, within the sea's interior, to symphonic glissades
I return to Kafka...and a whole string of radiant names

The sea is withdrawing...glints of knife-blades
Keep company with chromed reality...as dust settles
On city wall, great bridge, avenues, city lights
Each fits together with its kind, and the rooftops
Are a red expanse

(25.11.2017, afternoon, Budapest)

* *An early novella by the author Su Tong was titled A Crowd of Wives and Concubines. The poet Ouyang Jianghe is known for a long avaunt-garde poem he wrote in the early Nineties titled "Glass Factory." This line juxtaposes two utterly different approaches to literature: social critique and self-referential deconstruction of language.*

A CERTAIN ATTITUDE

The Danube River, having flowed this far, is tripped up by love
Buda presents itself obliquely, a timeworn aristocrat
Baring its bullet-riddled chest, and confides its sorrow to Pest

This secret can no longer be kept, the great bridge is magnificent...
In its banality; the imperial palace and the four seasons
Are engaged in an exchange of rocks, trees, statues
And pompous coats of arms, plus outdated tenderness
The Diet is a different kettle of fish...hearkens to far-off Fisherman's Fortress
Its structure is an ornate conch shell
In which only the clang of bells remains

Sunlight behind grapes gets bottled into wine
Greed heads off to the ends of the earth
Budapest has been laying plans for elopement
Though bleary and tattered, should it return to the imperial center
Its symphonies that were partitioned off
Would outdo any kind of banquet

(26.11.2017, morning, Budapest)

WEIGHT OF A SPONGE

When you hold a youthful ideal in your arms
The weight of a sponge is the weight of wings
When lovers are loath to part from each other
When the waves of your career rise chest-high
When fruit trees have to flower and bear fruit
The weight of a sponge is the weight of flying
When seashells have to wash ashore

When tides have to ebb and flow
When April cherry blossoms have to open fully
The weight of a sponge
Is the weight shifted from the left hand to the right
When the American continent was destined to be discovered
When fingernails are destined to grow
When Bruno was destined to be burnt alive
The weight of a sponge
Is the weight of one gram of grey matter
When breasts are destined to fill out
When vultures are destined to desolation
When desert and oasis are destined to co-exist
The weight of a sponge
Is the weight of a patch of cloud
In everyone's heart, the weight of a sponge
Is the weight of the blue sky
The weight of the sea
The weight of the air
The weight of the blood
Of one heart yearning for another

A MANTIS SITTING IMMOBILE

A mantis crouching in an aged pose
Its green blood still clear and bright
Countless details that I can bring to mind
Are like this fish skeleton shining before my eyes
Opening the mailbox, mail of decades
Is piled high in the heart's storehouse
A lover at his last gasp
Lacks strength to pound on the door

The cottage inside a hedge of cigarette butts
Has wrapped itself with padding of smoke
In the season of blossoming fireworks
As green fragrance wafts through air
The mantis is like my dry-as-straw hair
Its thin legs shrinking bit by bit
The brown season has mounted to its green eyes
Dearest aged mantis
My heart is full of wrinkles
Could we perhaps join hands and
Spend some lovely hours together?

My palms are leaves split by wind and rain
Once on a sunlit platform, like no other woman
My feet were suffused with light, like your body
Now the roots are aged, the vines rotten
Ringing notes of song grow intermittent

Mantis, mantis
Hold that colored pencil while you have strength
And crawl into my mailbox fringed with greenery
I stand beside the hoary, white-haired street
Getting a view of the light

A HEAVILY-LADEN LETTER HOME

I send you a whole house
Dearest Dad and Mom
Gathered here are four years of my breaths
All my hardships and tears given time to dry
And I have meticulously wiped the melancholy dust

Are things at home OK?
That patch of blue sky, fresh spring onions in the backyard
And those gorgeous yellow day lilies in summer
Dad, Mom, are you reconciled to my leaving you?
Your glad laughter putting up poles in the bean field
Father wordless in the field of silent rapeseed
Now what do I have but this unhealthy house?
I cannot harvest neon of the city and send it to you
I cannot tie up a bundle of prosperity
I am your frail and thin daughter, just as always
The only pictures I sent showed me wearing a city coat
Are the curved garlic sprouts still a lustrous green?
Are thick-growing green peppers still bent at the stem?
I am most concerned for the sapling planted when I left
Has it grown into a pear tree full of flowers and foliage?

Mom
Have you forgotten the quarrels
By the oil lamp that held back dark night at the riverbank?
I harbored ideals, wouldn't listen to your admonitions
Wouldn't step into life along the track you devised for me
Or fly into the sky within the picture you drew for me

Yet now I am tired beyond endurance in a far city
My onetime ideals have faded and ebbed away
The reasons for our quarrels do not matter now
Mom, forgive me
Will you quarrel with me again for all those things?

Days of flying golden sparks are hidden close to my chest
Sad clouds of painful, helpless hours are clutched in my hands
I want to grow into my father's tree, my mother's flag
Dad, Mom, I am decorating this small house for you
Before I put it in the mail
I will paint it a brand new color
I will want you to feel proud of the healthy plants
Next to the far field, in the gorgeous evening glow

Yet you cannot know, after mailing the little house
Alone in night, I will be immersed in coldness
Ending up immobile in the air over the city
Like a homeless cloud

SODERGRAN

Sitting on a Las Vegas balcony, I watch the sparkling revelry
Of last night, now going dim in the heaven of my senses
Yesterday through a porthole at San Fransisco Airport
I watched planes like graceful whales come and go at dawn
Turning around to look back
I saw you, after passing through a century
Still holding a lyre, sitting tranquilly at the feet of God
And singing like an angel

You are part of the heavenly ladder
Thorns and flowers were on the road you walked
What once stabbed you is still stabbing us
What you once sang of we sing in your footsteps
Yet we no longer have lyres
Here on this flourishing ruin
We can return to your roses and stars
Only with help of dreams, impelled by you
Countless readers breathe in fragrance
From the petals you let fall a century ago
Your hunger and cough
Have become nutrition for poetry
As far as possible, we chase a deer in the wasteland
Only for the moment of collision
With your lingering glance from a century ago

BAUDELAIRE

You sucked all prostitutes' breasts and turned them into wizened oranges
You wrung their arms dry
You saw a profusion of maggots
Crawling everywhere upon a big, luxuriant tree
You sang loudly on a branch tip
In a voice that rang through the 19th century

You squandered goodness just like money
Those sickly flowers along the Paris streets
Were an affront to the eyes of moralizers
Tapping your walking stick
You selected women
As objects to vent your spleen

And so, you crawled like that
Crawling toward a beautiful cat
For whom you felt unbounded tenderness
In the end, Baudelaire
You had to fall into your mother's arms
Let the beginning become the end
And the end become the beginning

YFAN GOLL

Snuff out your dimples
Snuff out the homesick road
Snuff out the tenderness of steel pipe
Snuff out bloodlines
Snuff out your mad dash down the road
Snuff out you

Then nothing is left you but poetry itself
Like a naked scorpion
Poisoning my whole body
I wish to die in your tenderness
And be reborn a hundred years later
To live happily
As an unremarkable grasshopper

(24.06.2011, Evening)

ACHILLES

I want to become a stone in your grand tragedy
Or a hair on a Trojan girl's head
Or a hair from a pore on your bicep
Or a drop of water which changes
Into your tear the moment you fall

You have no tears
The Lord says a hero's blood is a river of history
Achilles
You lived for an era of heroes
For the flash of swords in countless battles
For the destruction of Troy
For great conquests and pointless vanity

"I fought battles all my life
It is you who gave me peace."
The peace that the beautiful Trojan princess longed for
Is your sea of happiness
Achilles
Your stillness is an era's stillness
Your end is an era's end

Your valor has turned into wishfulness
The world is rife with worms
Trees and sky draw unhealthy breaths
Achilles
Luckily you fell in the environs of Troy
Or your restless temper would become a lance
That would pierce the heart of another age

IMAGINING QINGHAI *

Summer will soon be over
Restless ardor is receding
The sky becomes azure like Kokonor Lake
Songs are loud and clear
Far away like Guernica in Picasso's memory

A girl gallops by on horseback
Bound for a rendezvous with the plain
A beard grows out bristle by bristle
O, prince of Qinghai
The lake is your heart, pitching its bosom-full
Of lofty immensity
O Golmud
The bonfire is lit amid flying sands
Whereupon a holy robe is taken off
The unbelieving boy who entered your skin
Who once overlooked your shoulders
Now sits in upright posture at home
Distant Qinghai
I am the young wife in your painting of summer

It turns out you are totally empty, dear one
You have the purity of thin air, with your broad brow
Pillowed on the Heavenly Railway
Tibet is your distance, your future
Your beloved, the palm of your hand

You are a dream of passing pilgrims
Qinghai
On one side are sunlit snowy mountains
On the other is sadness of the interior
Your love is always on the way

Take a handful of sand
It can multiply into a beach
Which has to do with your life
Inciting a tree to fear and reverie
At night, a big cat of Qinghai enters your dream
And prowls through your housing development
With graceful, lordly reserve
Small trees join to make a forest
And big trees become history
While I
Become a lion crossed in love

(08.06.2008)

* *Qinghai is a large province in China's far west. It is home to grasslands, deserts, and the northern part of the Qinghai-Tibet Plateau. Within its boundaries can be found Qinghai Lake (Kokonor) and the sources of three major rivers: Yellow River, Yangtze River and Lancang (Mekong) River.*

FINANCIAL CRISIS

Shaken banks collapse, paper money flutters
The stock market does a high dive
Confidence is a sinking boat

Guns are in people's hands
But the people can find no enemy
Golf has fallen into a collective hole
There is pleasure in swinging a club
Yet for the likes of Wall Street traders
All swings miss the ball

California sunshine cannot drive away the cold
Golden Gate Bridge is littered with corpses
The famous island prison emits a cold light
Innovation
is made to wear a ridiculous cap

Our small town's apples are unsaleable
Migrant workers come home ahead of time
The white tiger of the south has died
The whole world has caught a cold

The cruise ship has lost its compass at sea
An iceberg
meanders through a late night of 1912
Pool all the credit of mountains and seas, with vows
Rated by value of birds flying skyward
And pray that the sun
Will rise as ever tomorrow

(15.11.2008)

DESPOTIC MORNING

Willing or not, I must awake
You part the night's curtain, perfectly on time
Sweeper-trucks spray water, too impatient to wait

Assembly lines move around the clock
Cocks crowing and dogs barking
A steady stream of horses and carriages
Such a despotic morning

Eager breaths of the morning's glow
Sunbeams reach into my sleeping bag
The city's body is shedding its talons
In scorching summer, dreams grow anemic

Such a despotic morning
I step into the swimming pool
Hold my breath a good while, climb the edge
Right before my eyes I see
A high-end luxury skyscraper
Slumping to the ground

(16.07.2012)

DAGGER

An empty noun, suspended
In the air
Like a crime in free fall
Son of iron, its shape
Is the only topic

Its shape offers evidence
The head evades the heart
Vegetables play dead under knives
And genuine animals
Remain expressionless
With a noisy roar, the dagger
Puts an end to itself

(04.07.2012)

HUNGER

Food and I, at two different ends
Of a carrying pole or a suspension bridge or a heavenly road

This long, long shoulder pole
The long stretch of this suspension bridge
And the heavenly road so endless

My stomach is an empty sea
My intestine a cliffside walkway
Vertigo a hand's breadth away
Afloat
In the last drop of water

(16.07.2012)

LAN

The imposing lintel has been recorded
The ring symbolizing power and honor
has been inherited
The heavy gate opened to ensuing generations
The genealogy printed on the blood of the clan
A sequence extending into the future

A river flowing and flowing
A breath relayed forward
A gene inherited

Ancestors are lonely
With one keystroke they have been relegated
Into their grandchildren's internet games

Which does not affect the clan's propagation

(27.05.2011)

THE ORCHID'S WILL

Bring a journey to its end
Bring loud snores under control
Coolness stretches
along the seaside. A cucumber
Decomposes under flowers

The intention of greenery could never be thus
The orchid has a well-thought-out plan
But a key may rust
On the way home
One scandal succeeds another
Sterling conduct and character
Have become antiques

The orchid becomes discolcred
In betrayal it hesitates

(04.07.2012, Night)

MUSIC FROM A HORSE'S HOOVES

A sandstorm envelopes the Great Wall
Dense fog rolls in from Mongolia
Ambiguous Beijing is too jaded
To show a smile
The horse
Has flown over Western Hills
Its reins dragging on Chang'an Avenue

Exhibitions big and small squat in halls
Operas convulsing and gabbling
Notes of a cello soured by car exhaust
While the singer
Has burst out sobbing
In the chaotic stable

The horse has flown
Through airspace over the capital city
Colored glaze broken
A horse's hooves drumming
The Forbidden City empty
The GDP is soaring
A dizzy-headed bunch of think-tank experts
Are swinging bell-clappers
Each sticking to his own position

Bubbles bursting on the city's outskirts
The horse   flying over the grassland
New-style fodder is awarded at the Great Hall of the People

The wasteland
Is awash with fear
A horse's hooves drumming
Like Don Quixote
Singing his heart out

(06.07.2012, evening)

ANTS

They are used to lightning and thunder outside the cave
As for those with direct experience
Their corpses are strewn across the open country
Tree branches toss in the rain
Terror of ants
Comes from muggy solitude

Frogs sing in the rain
Funeral dirges of ants

Rain still falls
No way to escape
Flags are short on oxygen
Before the fireplace heats up again
Another threat descends unnoticed

Ants are fasting and praying
Before the plum rains

(04.07.2012)

CAPTIVATION IN THE MIRE

A tongue licks the cup's rim
Food for a lifetime grows in the bowl
Springwater and petroleum
On that side of a life-engulfing mire
Fruitfulness
Results from plunder

Don't catch and break a man's heart once again
Captivation at the rubbing of shoulders
During a decorous dinner party
Heaven in a duel with earth

Such a solid mire

(16.07.2012)

SHALLOW DOVES

Fragments of time scrape my feet
My bones are hollow
You hear me make sounds
As I take flight

My sight is limited
In front of the profound lion
I am as insubstantial as paper
Before the storm comes
Each falling feather
Is my signal of peace

(09.06.2012, morning)

SANSHA CITY

All entanglements you can imagine
Are here
Games with complicated designs
Are boiling at high temperature
Sansha
This country and that
Stamped on flags
Raise outcries

Fists fall into the sea
Aircraft carriers peer and prowl
Torpedoes shuttle through dim depths

Fishermen pretending to be in high spirits
Warily put out to see

Sansha is a hunk of meat torn many ways
Schools of fish converge in displays of strength
The flabby economy
Needs strengthening by war

Just as your fingers need not clasp together
Until you run into an enemy

(16.07.2012)

COMMERCIAL NEGOTIATION

Suppositions extend in an exchange of words
Hands probing into brains,
Get hold of intelligence, experience and sparks
To be concocted into a statement
In the push and pull of revision
There is a tug-of-war for benefits

Red wine is imbibed on the face
White liquor is excitement of the blood
Goblets are interspersed with stratagems
As lustrations for a tacitly knowing handshake

A beach
Grows on paper
Wind brings spermatozoa of God
Flowers bloom and fruit grows

(16.07.2012, early morning)

PIRANHA

Close the door to avoid
Pursuing fins
Blood flows away in imagination
Fear infiltrates
Through the crack of the door

You chomped right through a steel hook
Right through fingers
At the head of your troop
That can engulf a whole cow

Bovine bones float in water
Your teeth are armed music
Nothing stands in their way

(11.07.2012, Qinhuangdao City)

NETWORK

People lead their lives in fiber-optic cables
Their joy and happiness, their sadness
Or else thievery and sinful acts
Heaving heavy sighs

Cold optical fibers heat up due to rapid messages
People have secret affairs, riding on light beams
A lifeless state, in handcuffs
The culprit-mouse cannot chew
Time. The man hurling curses
Has his own private glee

A maggot, finally grown into a pale and pudgy son
Clutches a stale loaf of bread
Like his honest father who holds a timeworn brick
Against his chest

No more stars and moonlight
Birdsong and cricket chirps will become dreams
Human beings, amid hurrahs for new technology
Die collectively
In a big net

(09.06.2012, morning)

MAY

an elegy for Second Uncle

Your invisible hands touch grass roots
Branches toss over earthen field dividers
Wheat stubble burns in the fields
Golden month of May
Wearing its cape of heatwaves
Allowing death to happen in secret

Roadside wormwood crept up to the door
Medicinal leaves were burned, rendering up life's fragrance
Glutinous rice balls dropped into gruel
Chopsticks were choked and shedding tears

Reeds beneath trees still grow crazily
A cortege of wailers tramps
Pine branches are thrown in the fire
May
Ants change their dwelling
You, growing in the field
By means of your grandson's lantern
Can also feel autumn, winter
Spring and summer

(09.06.2012)

THE VERTIGO OF FOUR LIMBS

A tongue of pale blue flame
Is hidden in alcohol
Dull thunder borrowed from far mountains
Insinuates itself into annoying music
Drowsiness reels and meanders
Through prickly heat left by the daylight
A nightgown floats down
From before the windowsill
From upstairs
Comes creaking sounds of lovemaking

The sun has scorched the moon
In the summer night   limbs are in a trance
Numbness spreads through the body
Dense smoke is drawn out from its sheath

Intertwining love is daubed with ashes
A city
Sinks beneath water

(16.07.2012)

AN ENGLISH NIGHTGOWN

A piece of cotton cloth
Enfolding a touch of amorous Albion
Floated here across the sea

Time displayed in the British Museum
Flows along the nightgown's hem
Smoke from history's tobacco pipe
Wreaths around an empire's mouth

With no end of amorous wiles, the owner
Takes time stretching her slender waist
Scotland and England beside the bed
Nuzzle up against the cotton gauze

Love from the nightgown
Pours forth all the while

Upon that robe sleeps
The morning of England

(16.07.2012)

MENSTRUATION

Blood   flows on rocks
Layers of sandy soil   straw
Woody fibers
A seed has missed
The hotbed
Drip drop, the tip of a girl's braid
has fallen into the hinterland

Millstone turning for a thousand years
River and time
Have an eternal appointment
Fertile loam of a woman
Womb
Streak of morning glow

(04.07.2012)

CUPPING TREATMENT

Gasket of my breast
Thousands of soldiers and horses on my back
Bioenergy goes coursing
Through an airless pottery vessel
Applied by a formless hand
A technique akin to scraping

Blood   flowing through my abdomen
Heart   falling into the wilds
The jungle across the back's expanse
Is laid low
Clay cups are applied
All over my body
This palimpsest of wounds
is recovering

(16.07.2012)

ROLLING THUNDER

Waves of heat
Roll across the wild
The hollow conscience
Is thumping and trembling

In a cavalcade
This chaotic mass
Of neighs and tossing manes
The general and the marshal
Meet in the rain

(04.07.2012, evening)

WOUNDED WOLF

Grief and outrage
Pour outward from your wounds
Each of your blood-red hairs
Documents days of slaughter in the wild

Wails arise from depths of those green-glinting wells
A weathered smile tells tales of hard-won ease
Famine, chill, arrogance are knobs on the staff
That props your faith: you will never meet defeat

Used to death   used to willful abuse of the soil
That is made to soak up gouts of blood
Yet you possess dark forests scored by ravines
Dark forests
Growing from the land like tenacious whips
Under leadership of your high-raised tail
Preying and being preyed upon

Amid brutality, the raspy buds on your broad tongue
Filter out and easy-going kindness toward your kind
But from wrestling with your rages, for five thousand years,
The stalwart of this land has flesh riddled with scars
Strokes dashed off by your inkbrush, soaked in black blood,
Pierce the paper's soul quickly, but with rapt absorption

Whirling wind blows your horn of sorrow
The ever-changing eddies hunt down wild ghosts
And chase the shepherd who lost his loincloth

A bird comes flying...its call sounds like dripping blood
With a red banner hanging from its beak—"God of the Wild"
Singing all the way

NAKED BATH

Leaves and petals
Like floating hoofprints
Innocence and nobility of a nine-color deer
Jade-like and exquisitely featured

Soft smoothness of warm spring-water
Caresses the skin like fine silk cloth
A thicket
Where thousands of leopards are dashing
Over the abdomen with a rolling motion

Crystalline knolls
Topped by pink stamens
Red flush   ripples gaining ground
Bashfulness and plump ripeness
A pool strewn with floating rose petals

ROARING CASTLE

A double-barreled shotgun was just taken from the wall
Its breech still closed upon a pockmarked bore
When folks who threw firecrackers at each other for fun
Hear a ferocious roar from the bowels of the earth
This mountain-top castle, hundreds of meters high
Trembles as if suffering from malaria
Humans and animals begin to flee
The mortared bathing pool is indecisive

As if thousands of troops are assembling
Fast-running feet are gauging the explosion's edge
Fine sand is ready to throw itself into cracks
An ever-lasting second

***

Lava begins to spurt
The castle becomes a dragon-mouth
An ocean of flame
Is spewed into the clouds

Instantly the Earth shakes
Fowl and beasts are driven off by heat waves
Notes of a flute are swallowed in the roar

***

The land gapes in wide-eyed amazement
Old trees, scorched by fire, stare at flying rocks
Watch them fall into innocent water
Eventually, everything calms down
The castle, extinguished in nirvana
Holds out its majestic walls
Cooled lava droops on the rampart
Like a towel for feet of the Almighty

I lie dreaming of peaks flattened and seas upended
And witness a volcano going through my heart
Jutting against the sky-vault which sheltered our ancestors
Then raining down from high above
Scorching the canopied bed of memory

PRISONER

for B

Your teeth were cracked from grating in fury
So you could no longer ruminate on freedom
Your pride in full bloom
Strewed its petals heroically on the ground
You strove to maintain composure to the end
Yet household banalities piled straws on your back
Your arms once gestured at ways to reshape our world
Now they strike against houseflies and written words
Like a lion kept in a cage

Perhaps you are using your time behind bars
To erect a virtual Great Wall
But your blood cools down
Those you love and those who love you are at a loss
Those you hate and those who hate you have no opponent
A broken smile fails to cover your heart's bitter tears
Sunshine outside the window
Is your sole view
In your own way
You bid farewell
To everything outside the walls

MID-AUTUMN

I can only greet you in such a manner
As you illumine green hilltops overhead
And with the passion that lines my raincoat
When the moon is full
I take cover in a reedbed
The reed tassels resemble your trailing beard
I hide in a jug of old rice wine
Somewhere on mirror-like Qingxihu Lake

Perhaps, you'll give in to fond recollections
Those days of clear, bright water
Are sprinkled through my sleepless nights
Like sparkling stars
From Dragon Boat Day to Mid-Autumn Festival
A lifetime's endearment keeps company with the moon

You will never be swallowed up
The sun and moon rotate in turn
You sit on a brilliant mountaintop
Sharing revelations of passing seasons
In pure beams of light

PASSING BY THE TOWN OF WANGCAO (THRIVING GRASS)

Red bayberries leave the tips of branches
To extend their youth in medicinal liquor
Clover on a hillside
Is enamored of golden rice-fields
When you pass by, kernels are growing plump
You uproot weeds from field dividers
To hear the trickle of irrigation water
Then you go to a village
To replace the old, run-down flagpole
It gladdens you to see smiles
Appearing on the farmers' faces
Yin Zhen's presence seems to linger in the hall*
Holding dialogue with us across time and space
In this thriving little town, early autumn
Soaks up sunlight, like a well-tended orchid plant
Upon your broad, square shoulders

**The scholar Yin Zhen (76-162 A.D.) transmitted humanistic learning to Guizhou Province, thus establishing connection with the civilization of the Central Plain.*

SCUBA DIVING

Encountering a sea lion
Its whiskers kissing water plants
Slight sound of motor on the surface
A boat entering the bay

Placid self-containment of coral
Causes anxiety for the distant crocodile
It is a thinker
Studying the power of teeth and conspiracies

Before going under
I contemplate a piece of wood steeped for years
Shaped by the sea, permeated with salt
Like the weight of many seasons

Shoals everywhere
Territory of fishes
Before they grow fins
They have learned to puff water
To deal with fully-armed humans
They have only naked beauty
Do away with these flippers
And dive into another stage of life

NIGHT MEAL

There comes a time for pouring vinegar on potatoes
As if their innocence were not worth a cent
Forgetting the joy the tongue once took
In just an olive, or a nipple
Yams and corn mush went together so well
As if still in the field
A stir-fried dish
Is now condoned as a third party
After eating up
Bowls and chopsticks are thrown into a basin
The lamp is snuffed out
As if nothing happened

JERUSALEM

This ragged diamond
Each facet reflects an eerie light
The slaughters you recorded
Highlight the innocent and unstained lamb
Road of the Cross
through walking becomes a pilgrimage

As always you adorn yourself with cheap accessories
In this perverse city
Only weeping stones
Cracks upon cracks
Show the pain of God
Jerusalem, long ago broken up
And kneaded into the Bible
Via those wafers and communion cups
Like dust falling into the hearts of disciples
Seeds of renewal
Have taken root on a steadfast rock
Each and every one
Heading towards Heaven

When night descends
North wind howls in Gethsemane
Golgotha wails without cease
The Holy Sepulcher is empty
Leaving the tall cross shining
The light of redemption

THE IMPULSE OF A SEAT

You must not dig the tomb too deep
For angels may descend
The canopy will be torn at the center
The quaking mountain will shiver
And bare its two-thousand-year chest
A trailing beard will harken back
To the Exodus
On the path to Canaan
Where the Red Sea parted, a falling leaf
Could lead toward engulfing ruin

A heartbeat not relating to blood
Jesus
You pinch wheat-ears on the Sabbath
To anoint my heart with plumped kernels
Waves of Galilee
Keep washing over broken conch shells
On my knees
I hear sounds of you with fishermen
Painfully tightening a net
Your hand bloody from grasping thorns
Sweeps over chaotic Jerusalem
At the city's edge are outlanders
Who cried out in the wilderness
Holding straw sandals from the desert

I keep shedding tears
For the crab-tree misunderstood in summer

I walk through the Last Supper
And Gethsemane's never-ceasing prayers
That pervade an ethereal Dead Sea
with its heavy weight of mud

(20.08.2013, in Beijing)

BLY AT 4:00, BEFORE DAYBREAK

Bly at 4:00, before daybreak
Sends a late-fall mosquito to wake me
A square of dark chocolate
A donkey grabbed by the bristly ear
Bly spoke of the judgement received:
"one thousand years of happiness"

Then I start to learn "silence in the snowy field"
And search for Minnesota in scenery around me
I am afraid of rousing the snake that sleeps under grass
The sunniness and strength of Bly
Tug me away from the death of Jozsef Atilla
I am so afraid to touch Baudelaire's weariness
To uncover a poets' depression and despair
Bly, as cheerful and lively as a hound
Is licking my wounds blackened by words

Then I fear insomnia no more
Who'd think each word could serenely bring light
Bly's pirate ship from the opposite shore
Is fully loaded with fish and shrimp and jewelry
Then let my bread be spread
With the pride of a fisherman

CLEOPATRA

Your fine linen-covered body
Like Orient silk
Outmatching brigades of crack horsemen
Has dethroned so many dynasties
Your deep, kohled eyes
Are a vast territory
Stretching from Rome to Egypt
From the Nile to the Mediterranean
You took a gold coin
And conquered the head stamped upon it

As for those great souls
With their noble swords
From Caesar to Anthony
All melted on your lips
On your forked tongue

Heroes falling like blossoms
Brightened your tomb
And your repose
Love was a dream compounded
Of blood and tears
It outlived war and death
Surviving in your smile

INN

You can make the inn's lights dim down
Just by removing
Your numismatic coat
Squabbles are the real starvation
A lantern always shines to satisfy itself

A rafter breaks at the touch of a winecup
This inn
Is a mark made by your previous incarnation
Tiles hide fresh sawgrass
from view; the tavern keeper's mate
Rushes in bringing a note
A horse is on its way   to stay the night
The old roadway turns busy
Door planks are covertly excited
Between you and a void

In the café of your future incarnation
Some stories made of bricks will always happen
A cup of water shared   the boots that betray you
Pass straight through   while at the bar-counter
a hidden enticement is set in motion
Wait until the horse's owner
Assembles his troops and returns to court

QINGXIHU LAKE

I often miss you at my desk in Beijing
Facing the white wall, I close my eyes
So the window won't interfere with you
Sunlight and smog stop at the curtains
You float up from the bottom of my heart
Like a girl without face powder
Quietly showing your pale green purity

Rippling on this Valentine's Day morning
And if a puff of wind blows
That's your girlish wish, a suggestion of spring
In today's brisk and festive air

I've been hankering for the sanctity of Tibet
But I dislike rough winds that strew grit
Over robes and faces of believers
Your lovely looks are kept in an inner chamber
Your full head of fine, long hair
Your mouth holds a precious stone
At the doorway of heaven, like translucent jadeite

I know it won't do—simply to miss you from afar
If there is thunder
I will get an inkling
That you've sensed my fond thoughts
and sent a fish through the air
to deliver your answer

THE WORLD BEYOND HUMAN BEINGS

A lissome ostrich falls
To end its life in a leopard's mouth
Two male longhorn beetles
Compete for territory on a high branch
The female longhorn, used and abused
Is thrown down from the tree
The barbarous King lets out a yell
Holding high its pincers

A pretty dolphin swims on its back
Shows its white belly to the azure sky
A raptor catches a songbird in flight
While its fledglings squeak eagerly for food
Thousands of ants hold up leaves
Or flowers   as grand as an army column
A slim and graceful mantis
Is nabbed by a reptile's gummy tongue

A mountain goat leaps up a crag
Narrowly evading its cliffside predator
A pair of swans, deeply in love,
Dance a water ballet like no other
Fish swim an in enormous school
Which avoids big fish and swooping birds
Like a mobile, transformable artwork
An ancient elephant clan walks in the sunset
In a faraway place
A crowd of flying fish
Dash toward their dream on the sea

ONE DAY

One day
My manuscript will have turned into a relic
Amid a hubbub of voices
Words will sift down on a street in Jerusalem

One day
On the high plateau
The King will play the role of matchmaker
Betrothing me to the mountain prince
With the scarf on my head
I'll enwrap my marriage from a past life

One day
When I perish in an alien region
I'll embrace it as my lover's bosom
Silks will be strewn on the ground*
In cold wind

** The image of silks on the ground evokes the fate of Yang Guifei, favorite consort of the Tang emperor Xuanzong. When Anlushan Rebellion broke out, Emperor Xuanzong fled the capital with a small group of retainers and counselors. The group stopped at Mayang Slope, where the counselors held an emergency meeting. They blamed Yang Guifei for leading the emperor astray and demanded that she be strangled on the spot.*

YELABUGA
to Tsvetaeva

That was your own hook
That chewed the bitter wormwood to its end
Yelabuga
Red Russia
White Russia
Russia of ardor that permeated your blood
Russia so unfamiliar you couldn't draw near

That is your own mountain ash tree
Elderberries as dark as your blood*
Tsvetaeva
You left your high-point in Prague
Spent seventeen rootless, gut-wrenching years
Then you reached Yelabuga and thought
Overcoming loneliness would bring you love
Leaving homesickness would save your life
But that hook of desperation
Was on the rafter in Yelabuga
After 100 years I find you in hot, rolling tears

The last day of August, 1941
The sun was shining on your feet
Your curly hair was grass of the wasteland
You didn't know your husband and child
Would follow you so soon
Yelabuga got no taste of your blood

** The Chinese word for elderberry is jiegu-cao ("bone-setting herb").*

PULAU PANGKOR

I

Stripped down, until only the heart is left
Only wind and bellowing waves are left
Nobody to expound on bygone flames of war
At the banquet of the prince and his consort
Skin is so lightsome as to be translucent
Except for the sweeping arm of Pangkor
And the recurrent dream-babble
Which have become alluring lies
All-too-common on this isle

II

Sunlight slid along the bridge of your nose
While watching the water of Pangkor
I rose from the surf before your eyes
Like a pretty mushroom
I was almost blossoming
Forgotten was the saline taste of stars*
At the back of every breakfast

I recklessly drank a pungent glass of durien
You solicitously sent a rain-shower
At that moment
Wind tousled my cropped hair, whipped my skirt
At a turning place
An umbrella
Was opened

* *The word xingxing星星 in Chinese, meaning "stars," sounds the same as xingxing腥腥, meaning "fishiness."*

YOU AND I

Between you and me lies a rainbow
Also bees and wings
A forty-year wasteland and four centuries of savagery
Lord
Waters of the Red Sea have parted
You descend in the morning fog

I've gone astray in the treacherous desert
Like a grasshopper
With my faith gone lame
Wailing in the pitch-dark night
There was never a sword   only nails
Prick my heart all the way from Golgotha
Your thorns are burning
Your crown crushes a reed
You and I
Joined in blood on the cross
From that moment
You and I   melt into the light
Between us lie heaven's sanctum and a deep ravine
Allowing your revelations
To grow from my head

RETURNING IN DREAMS TO QINGXIHU LAKE

A doe passed this way last night
Her glance was tender like the quiet lake's surface
Water seeped into her hoofprints
Moonlight poured down
Little mandarin ducks are resting neck-to-neck

A prince comes drifting downstream
Steers his way into your silken bosom
A lithe and slender Milky Way
Stands above silvery scales

I am a smoothly contoured fish
In this night stretching vast distances
Water is only centimeters away

Might as well become like that silent pier
Or be wooden like the deck of a boat
Or dwindle down to pine-needle size
Become material for a raft built by ants, to drift
From Precarious Peak Bridge to Old-Crag Stream
Like a cricket drunken from taking in all that scenery
Find a mooring place at Seven-Star Island
And exchange shy glances with ducklings

It's alright if I never get sober again
Curl up in cotton flower for love of you
As long as your heart remains like jadeite
In a cliff-side waterfall, in mossy rocks
I will watch over you another 100 million years

SUIYANG IMPRESSIONS

Standing at the tip of a bamboo stem
I come swooping down before you
In this range of mist-wreathed mountains
On this path through burgeoning wildflowers
On where can I wash this ceruse from my face
Without soiling the pure greenness of your blouse?

Sandstone from 400 million years ago
Watches over life's ongoing chain
Oh water-hollowed cave of Twin Rivers
You await me with marvelous stonework
Your mysteries that cannot be uttered
Have reached me in deepest nighttime
Drawing close to Qingxi Lake's stillness
I sense her pristine, verdant heart
Ah Fairy Maid, in such endearment
Lies the meaning of my rugged treks so far

A torch still sparkles amid far-stretching mountains
A man leads his group on night-and-day travels
Through this area of land, for the sake of its future
His eyebrows are wet with dewdrops
A soft leaf adheres to his shoulder
So many stars, touched by such actions
Add sparkle to these mountains and lakeside forests
A resonant and rousing song
Passes through the graceful restraint
Of a dream

WILDERNESS

That is where an arrow is about to be loosed
A place for coming across diamonds
A place for a hoof   from nails in its hornlike heart
To its coralline gleam
Birds are dying, breathing weakly
Moses' forty years of determination and gloom

That is where an ocean disappears
Honey grows from the thorns
Salt grows from a staff
Faith from a stone
Rebellious insects search for a glimmer of light
Wilderness where a roaring river
Rolls over the back of an injured horse

That is where the tender-hearted deer cries out
The homeless otter seizes a crab's claw
Breaks it against a willow branch where spring's greenness
Sends out new shoots
From bloodless corpses

JOB

You emerge erect from my root
Once again a great patch of decay flowers
Where disease after disease
Claimed my loved ones one by one
You string my tears into a chain
I strike the earth
As Moses struck the rock

A spring gushes from stone
You can take my last piece of clothing
As you'd reap a field's last stalk of wheat
my blood is the last honeydew
Take it too, if you wish
But please leave me the last dawn
Leave me my bitten, swollen lips
Leave me my teeth, chewing the frosty wind

I will arrive in Bethlehem ahead of time
To become a pliant stalk of hay in a manger
Or, failing that, some thirty years later
I will arrive in Jerusalem ahead of time
To pluck the spines from your crown of thorns
And become another Simon, shouldering your cross
Or another Magdalene
Preparing agar-wood and myrrh
To anoint your road-weary feet

This is my belief
Do not test me further, give me a bowl of water
I will make of it the river you require

BIRDCAGE

Is this a palace for a bird? You even gave her
A candlestick carved with flowers, a winning expression
As if the two of you share
The boundary between confinement and freedom
Are resignation and a tacit understanding
The qualities you long for?

That is a transaction of green and pink, as spring comes
To a courtyard beside the Qinhuai river with the sound of lutes and singing girls
A glamorous chamber-pot has been thrown down from the balcony
Night-time is rendered as a pitch black sheet
As if the bird's fine feathers could make us
Forget its rotten droppings
You paint the nights red so that nothing but light
Is important to you and that bird

KAFKA

My existence has become suspicious
In Prague you pass through streets and alleys
Like a beetle on my trail
I won't be able to walk back through the snow
A carriage went by as darkness fell

I went to the castle to visit you, to every place
You called home; I sought out your grave
Dora was there ahead of me
Even K. was there, at that oppressive place
Constantly distracted
You were a chronic insomniac
Your father, unable to foresee your triumph,
Snorted derision

I would not put you on trial
Even if you had taken all the beauties in Prague
On your sash is written: Frightened Soul
Jump into the grave, Dora
Death is an event
More ordinary and more dependable than life.

LURCHING FOREST

Carrying as dowry a castle, Denmark and a small stone
I dig a canal and marry Norway
This field of tossing waves displays a blue
Deeper than your eyes
The Baltic ploughs the ancient forests
Changing the soil on my breast
To an amber nugget veined with homesickness

Norway sits within a vanished song
With a book in its hands still drifting
Through my dim dreamscape
From the moment I boarded this ship, pirates
Have become my loved ones, and all the jewels
Are so salty they make me cry

MID-AUTUMN-SELF-PORTRAIT

I have torpedoed myself
That frolicsome moon
Has never called itself pure
Yet it is more elevated than you imagine

I am my own brother
I am the gap in the city's facade
I should not be a burden to my own shadow
Mid-Autumn on a distant lake
Invades a beautiful love story

Of course, this year on the aeroplane
Brings me closer to the moon; at 10,000 meters
I am frozen in panic. O Frida
And Salome, please use your stories
To warm the outer skin of this great bird

I am my own pair of scissors
From the roots of my facial hair
I learn to plough

Learn from that Bohemian lion
As of today, learn to be a poet
Do things you find absurd
No need to explain

Then with a pair of hazy shoes dangling from my fingers
I will drink all the way to Rome

HUAI'AN DUMPLINGS

Water of the canal makes you tender and translucent
Seeking intimacy with the tongue
You pass by the lips and teeth
They are a double door you've broken down
One side sensual, the other solid

Centuries ago, you were all the rage in the ancient town downstream
Your skin the curtains of a young lady's room
Myopic scholars pressed against it
Filling their heads with rouge and literature

With the twist of a chopstick
Your soul was clad in a trailing robe
The joy conveyed by busy hands
Contrasted with the sensation in your mouth

Empty pockets when I was young
Were no defence against your subtle assault on my nostrils
I had only to sniff your fragrance
And my saliva would outdo the river outside my door

UP IN THE AIR

I

Busy days
Sitting on a leaf, travelling
Into the mountains to drink with the moon

The mountain road shows dimly in starlight
The land resting from daylight toil holds deep warmth
The hum of insects is the only song of this forest
Between trees and numbers
The silence grows sweet

II

Mountain hollows are filled with fog
Like the snow in early spring refusing to let a dragonfly alight
Keeping it flying along the mountain ridges
In the depths of night you will find a household
Receptive to the traveller's heart

A drowsy pigeon
Is roused by the glimmer of a toadstool
As fog spreads like drifting snow
Mountains lose their edges, eagles
Lose direction
Unspun cotton balls are thick like wave crests
No solid bank a passing boat could moor at

III

Ridged spines of crocodile, bodies lurking in fog
Water drains away
Many dusky brown bluffs
Like the distant past where no one sets foot
To one who has flown in repeatedly in circles
Scales and crests of waves
Reveal their savagery

IV

This is a journey that didn't work out
A leaf after all is nothing to feel sorry for
This mountain is a sharp horn laid across the land
In a mouldy Chinese painting
Authentic but no longer friendly

Sunlight shines at changing angles through the porthole
Patience is a sheet of paper growing steadily thinner
Looking as if a breath or tap might tear it

V

A narcissus blooms on the crown of the head
Tassels in the hand sweep over a yellowed photo
Trailing sleeves are arcing back and forth
Cloud-walking steps cover miles in the blink of an eye
A tragicomic life is enacted on a little stage
Resplendent stagecraft of our operatic heritage
Eases the widening spiral of anxiety

The beautiful scenery is like food that has lost all savour
The jet plane circles like a donkey turning a water wheel
I cannot bid farewell to the fish with a light heart
There is no water in the sky
We are in the belly of a bird
At last the signal comes that we may land

WOOD AND HORSEHAIR

I

Have you seen the river
that runs through this forest?
I am like a wild horse
Pursuing light that sifts through branches
At sundown I am entwined in the sun's last rays
Like a poignant love-song
Ringing through the night

That was when I met you
You laid claim to a whole prairie
You were the prodigal son, fluffing your plumage
Magically ploughing wild fields beside the river
In this life how many fiery songs must I sing
To cover up the weakness I feel inside?

II

A tiger has been pursuing me
Through mirrors, through fantastic dreams
I dash through a forest, brought down at times
By hidden snares
I did not know what wine was
But I tasted all the mountain fruit
Until I met you and for the first time
Began to worry about the world.
An eagle took wing
Gliding over a world I had not seen

I saw a lovely whale leap from the sea
And heard an axe's blow beneath the surface
An axe cuts into water, chops through moss
It chops apart a nest of bees

I hear the sound of falling tears

III

How can I, in a patch of lotus stalks,
Find your breathing, your seed pod, your greenness?
Your thread of love that can't be cut off
Forgive me for once having trampled on your smile
In my chirping you once walked to the world's edge
There were times of reaping, crisp and diaphanous
You overlooked the wrinkles, the conflagrations
The rain showers were always
Exactly what was needed at the time

Have I ever lost direction?
Wearing a conical straw hat I protect myself from moonlight
I want to sing a song all the way out to sea
But you, my dear, are like a lovely mushroom
Still growing in my forest
I won't go far, I am here on the neighbouring mountain

You see my smog, my scales, my weeping heart

IV

Will I find you at last in a heap of piano notes?
In the rhythm of drumbeats, in the press of a milling crowd
In the mutual need and torment of wood and horsehair
Like the sobbing strains of love
Hearing pain in each other's souls
I sit erect in a bottle
Eager to see your untainted smile

That is your prairie, my dear
On your mountain peak you were reborn as a queen
Dew is your ambrosia, roses your cuisine
I am like a grimy beggar
On your clean white back I leave a noble footprint
I know you are deeply in love with me
As I know I cannot live without you

V

At last angels have descended among us
For which I kneel and thank all mountains, rivers, deserts and marshes
And kneel to all stars, twinkling or dark
Even to mosquitoes that vex me endlessly
I give thanks to all living wood
And a horse that no longer exists
I let go of the tiger in my heart
And begin to embrace the whale
I am embedded in a song
In some high place far away I knock to enter

MID-LIFE PATCHES

A thief pretending innocence
Has reached out to filch your orchard fruits
A foul smell drifts by a lonely apron
Unknown to you a hornet stings your hat
Not until next season will you know
That the thief has left you nothing but a hollow

TERRA-COTTA WARRIORS

You force open the windows, letting in sunlight
To gleam on the tops of our heads
We are brave warriors, invincible
Now you have made us
Into a pack of do-nothing clowns
For an endless stream of gawkers to admire

We refuse to bring our colours to you
For millennia in company with the Qin ruler
Under quiet ground our lives have rung
With sounds of the army, sounds of horses
Not even a horse's windblown mane can hide
From the eyes of arrows
The emperor's dream of immortality has come to pass
Like the code to the Egyptian pyramid
Hidden within the ear of a pharaoh
In a place of coiled serpents
Each molecule of air could cause countless casualties
The Qin ruler has a date with them, or so I hear
From the uncle of a eunuch's cousin
If you doubt my word, dig up the grave

Copied in figurines of clay or stone
We have been loaded in crates, shipped
In trucks, trains, planes and frigates we have never seen
While you head blindly towards disaster
About to face a crisis
We are car-sick, air-sick, sea-sick, tower-sick, smog-sick

You who trample and humiliate us like this
Can never have heard the Qin ruler's raging roar
Loud enough to collapse in the heavens and make foreigners shrink back
Only the despised sun-flag remains
The king's edict to stamp out your bloodline has been sent out
Some say that nine post horses have run themselves to death
You coward sons of bitches forsaken by your mothers
Just wait and see

In a war that had nothing to do with us
Xiang Yu made off with an entire armoury
Wretch, who borrowed with no thought of return
Finally cutting his own throat with his sword on the bank of Wu River
Yet you who have made nuclear weapons and clambered onto the moon
Wouldn't return us so much as a spear and a whip
And you hire a bunch of so-called experts
To reassemble the skeletons of my brothers

You must have been dazed by your poisonous smog
Don't blame us for that
The war underground has never stopped
Of course, it keeps clear of lava vents
And the underground singing and dancing have never stopped
Least of all next door
Where the concubine has often invited the great king
Our ruler seems to have lost his rigid notions of rank
And has been tempted by that plump peony of Chang'an
Some say his bed's canopy was torn by all their thrashing
We heard this, of course, from the godmother of the cook's granddaughter
Any tongue that spreads this rumour more widely will be cut out

Well, my grandsons, the day is breaking
Another day is starting with blank faces
To hell with ants and floodlights and all this smog
Everything you take to the grave with you
Makes you the enemy of the Qin palaces
We heard this from a stable groom
The paternal uncle of our colleague's father

MANDELA

You have finally become a fossil
Placed in a South African museum
Rays of light survived 27 years of confinement
Transforming a prince's dream
Into real-world mythology

Like a mole you delved into the underworld
Dived into tropical oceans teeming with fish
There were a few cold memo notes
A glimpse of rare mosses

Your skin colour was a message from God
The invasion that had started at the surface
Went on to swallow arid Africa
You could have been like your forefather
Who took twenty-nine wives, whose children
As numerous as hairs on a cow's tail
Were scattered, neglected, in tents across the desert
Just as your forefathers never knew
That the surface represents everything
So your descendants don't understand
How you were sold down the river
A history as bloody as a cleaver

LAY OUT YOUR UNREST

www.ingramcontent.com/pod-product-compliance
Lightning Source LLC
Chambersburg PA
CBHW020854160426
43192CB00007B/914
* 9 7 8 1 9 1 7 6 1 7 1 6 1 *